I0434843

BeYond The maSk

Shattering Porn Addiction

BeYond The maSk

Shattering Porn Addiction

By Larry Pierce

Copyright 2009 By Larry Pierce

All rights reserved, including the right to reproduce this
book or portions thereof in any form whatsoever.

1st Edition June 2009

For more information about the book, including sales
and permissions please contact the author at
www.rpa365.blogspot.com

Book design by Larry Pierce

Manufactured in the United States of America

ISBN 978-0-557-08115-8

Table of Contents

Dedication

This book is dedicated to God, Katie and Chris B. Thank you for helping to open my eyes to a life worth living, free from addiction!

About the Author

Larry Pierce grew up in the desert Southwest. He has a passion for life, God the creator and the outdoors. Married for over 16 years to Katie, she is the love of his life. They were a blind date set up by a mutual friend in 1991 and after dating for a year and a half they were married in Albuquerque, New Mexico where they lived for approximately 8 years before moving to the Denver area. Together they enjoy traveling abroad, four wheeling in the Rocky Mountains, dirt biking and exploring old ghost towns.

The idea behind the book is a result of many years of personally struggling with the addiction itself, in depth sexual addiction counseling, group therapy, understanding sexual addiction and a desire to help others know they are not alone in their fight with this addiction.

The author is not a sex addict expert nor a counselor and the contents of the book are his opinions and the plans for recovery discussed in the book are what best works for him.

For more info about porn / sex addiction, or to comment on the book, check out RPA365 Project at www.rpa365.blogspot.com.

Introduction

Iam a sex addict or what some would call a porn addict. This is a fairly new addiction coming out of the closet over the last 20 years or so and bursting onto societies scene as the onslaught of the internet has taken hold in people's lives. I am no expert or counselor in this field and this book is based on my opinions and my opinion for a successful recovery plan.

Addiction has gripped people and families, from all walks of life. According to industry experts, from the 1960's to the 1980's drug and alcoholism fought for the leading role among addictive behaviors in society. Therapists have helped put many tattered lives back together and divine intervention has helped many others and the purpose of this book is to help open our eyes about this addiction. To get the subject out in the open and the healing process started.

I was silent for many years, like a person locked in a cage with no key and no way out. Silently screaming and dealing with shame and tremendous guilt. I thought to myself, if there was just one person I could talk to and discuss this issue with, maybe they would understand and see things the way I have for years. Maybe, it would give me some kind of validation for what I felt inside. I wouldn't take that chance however. Like many people, the fear of being judged kept me from saying anything. What would people think I worried; yet it was slowly eating me up inside.

One day my wife, Katie, who has been right there with me through all this, mentioned counseling. I thought about putting all my stuff out there but I was fearful of going and discussing the issue with a so-called expert. What if it didn't work I thought? What if they didn't understand? However, going began a deep 24- month process of understanding this addiction, where it came from and realizing there is hope and freedom.

So, we ask, what is sex addiction? Patrick Carnes Ph.D defines this well by stating that "sexual addiction is an illness of escape. Its goal is to obliterate, medicate or ignore reality. It is an alternative to letting oneself feel hurt, betrayed, worry and most painful of all – loneliness. It is important to realize that the addiction itself is a solution to pain, past trauma and anxiety, the addiction literally becomes a coping mechanism. If somebody starts doing something to cope, and they do it long enough, the body adjusts to the point that it needs that level of activity just in order to feel balanced".

I hope this makes sense because when I first read this, it hit me like a brick! I mean, that was my life, coping with past sexual abuse, pain, anxiety, loneliness. Understanding this really did begin to open my eyes and see there are many people just like me. People in the sports field, business field, politics even pastors, all with a hidden side that most others do not know about. Porn is not the issue; it is the result of something much deeper. Like we discovered with alcohol and drug addiction, the addiction is the cycle of acting out again and again because of something that is skewed in our thinking. Addiction keeps us in this cycle. When we get stressed or taken out of our comfort zone we resort back to what we have always had, a safe place or safe haven. However addiction is not that at all. Usually the skewed thinking came from how we grew up and what was imprinted on our minds as children. Society says that porn is okay but porn addicts are not. That sex is great but sex addicts are not wanted. Thus you have a multi-million dollar industry that feeds on vulnerable people and is the cause of thousands possibly millions of addicts. A vicious circle of sorts that spins in on itself much like the addiction cycle.

There is hope, there is light at the end of the tunnel and through this book you will see that. What do we want for our future, continued imprisonment or freedom? Do we want to change or do we want to be sex addicts the rest of our lives? I actually had to say that to myself and lets face it, life is change and each moment is different from the next. We grow, mature and make decisions, some good, some not so good but hopefully we learn from our failures, our mistakes. You, like me, have probably heard this before but the first step is truly admitting you have an issue and accepting that issue and desiring to change the behavior. Change cannot happen before this crucial step of truly recognizing who you are. Once we get passed this point, we are on our way to discovering the freedom we want and desire so much. It took me awhile to accept I had an issue and actually say yes, I am a sex addict. I believe, that was because nobody wants to admit they have a problem. I think this is what we call pride and pride blinds who we truly are to ourselves.

Pride rises up and says we are not like this, we are better than this and no one can say different and even if they do, pride blinds us from listening to them. Pride makes us mad at them for what they say about us. We get self-righteous and proclaim "who do they think they are judging me like this"? But we have to get past this point of defensiveness, look our selves in the mirror and say "how is this working for me"? Is my life better with porn? Is my life better with the endless hours of drinking in the different images and trying to find that one perfect image? Is my life better spending all this money on dvds, magazines, porn sites just to get a glimpse of what I truly think is perfect?

The porn industry wants to suck you in, they want your money, that's how they survive! Think about it, what if you calculated all the money you have spent over the years, and instead you had saved that money. You, like me, would have a nice little nest egg for the future. But unfortunately life is not that easy and through several missteps that were or were not your fault you ended up here, like me, hooked on porn, hooked on sex and so obsessed with it that it was costing you your wife, your family, your job, your finances. We wind up wallowing in a toxic sea of guilt and shame and scream we will never do it again yet find ourselves back in the same place, spinning our wheels.

Maybe you've heard that "a time is discovered for every addict". What will your moment of discovery be? Will it be when you are cyber chatting with a so-called 14 year old girl, trying to hook up with her, only to find out when you are arrested that you were actually conversing with a police officer? Will it be when your son or daughter catches you in the act of masturbating to cyber porn images and they ask, what are you doing? Will it be when your wife sees you have been involved in an affair for more than a year and decides its over? Will it be when a close family friend drives past a massage parlor and spots your car and later confronts you about it? When will it end for you?

My time came when I was sucked so far in to porn that I was looking for younger and younger women to look at. I finally thought to myself, this is how sexual predators and child molesters are born, it has to be because I was thinking things that would freak most people out. Things like having sex with an eleven or twelve year old, or wondering what she looked like naked and trying to find those types of images. And other thoughts that scared me. These were not normal thoughts and it was then that I began to realize if I didn't get help soon, I would be headed down that path. The end would be in prison for committing a crime like child molestation. I didn't want to be labeled for life, as a pedophile or child molester and ostrasized by neighbors, family and friends.

So, we ask, "what's next"? Where do we go from here? We have to realize it's a journey from one place to the next, from addiction to freedom, from death to life.

My Problem-

I felt inadequate, unworthy, alone and afraid. My insides never matched what I saw on the outsides of others. Early on, I came to feel disconnected from parents, peers or myself. I tuned out with fantasy and masturbation. I plugged in by drinking in the pictures, images and pursuing the objects of my fantasies. I lusted and wanted to be lusted after. I became a true addict, sex with self, promiscuity, adultery, dependency relationships and more fantasy. I got it through the eyes, I bought it, I sold it, I traded it, I gave it away. I was addicted to the intrigue, the tease, the forbidden. The only way I knew to be free of it was to do it. "Please connect with me and make me whole"! I cried with outstretched arms. Lusting after the big fix, I gave away my power to others. This produced guilt, self-hatred, remorse, emptiness and pain and I was driven ever inward, away from reality, away from love, lost inside myself. My habit made true intimacy impossible. I could never know real union with another because I was addicted to the unreal and went for the chemistry, the connection that had the magic, because it bypassed intimacy and true union. Fantasy corrupted the real, lust killed love. First addicts, then love cripples, I took from others to fill up what was lacking in myself. Conning myself time and time again that the next one would save me, I was really losing my life.

Chapter 1

Addiction Concieved

Whoever said that life would be easy. Dave Letterman, Jay Leno?? I mean think about it. You come into the world a child, innocent and not knowing much about things around you. Parents are here to protect, teach and guide you as you get older but they are not perfect, are they? Little did we know as kids our parents had issues that came with them into their marriage and were handed down. Life is not easy, not a bowl of cherries, in fact far from it.

I grew up in what many consider a normal family, went to school, graduated in 1982 and love hard rock n roll. My favorite bands include Van Halen, Queensryche, Guns n Roses, Pink Floyd and the great Lynard Skynard! We loved seeing their concerts and hanging out afterward, racing cars and cruising what we considered our drag. I am a gear head as well and love the classic muscle cars. They were the hot cars of my generation. Most of what I have learned in rebuilding the cars I learned from my Dad. This is his hobby and over time, he taught it to me. I remember learning everything from bodywork to what kind of wheels and tires look good. I really enjoy it as there is nothing like seeing a classic muscle car restored to its former glory!

My mom and dad were like most parents, they can be protective and controlling. One instance I remember pretty vividly, when I was growing up was when I wanted to play drums in the school band. They wanted me to play anything else but them. So, I obeyed mom and dad and wound up playing piano and another time the trumpet. Not because I wanted to but because they said so. These instruments were not my passion and not what I wanted to play but the drums were, in fact I enjoy playing drums today. I took a few lessons, actually about 4 months worth and just fell in love with playing them. However in my family there were many times that these types of things happened.

I love basketball. The NBA rocks and is like my football season! Dwayne Wade, Shaq, Nash, Stoudemire, Billups, Spurs, Nuggets, Mavericks, oh, and the Final Four, it doesn't matter, I just love the game, these guys, the teams and the way they do their job! I loved it so much when I was a kid that you could find me on the weekend shooting hoops at the local playground or playing the game with friends who loved it as much as I did.

I began my freshman year in high school and like most kids entering high school, the butterflies were intense. As we began to settle in over the first few months, students would begin to make a name for them in whatever they chose to do. Some chose the debating team, golf, tennis, football or baseball. Most of my friends were trying out for football or baseball. Of course, I wanted to go for the basketball team. My parents had another direction.

Even though the desire of my heart was basketball and even though I loved it as much as I did, they wanted me to try out for track. Why?? I asked my mom. Because, your Father ran track, my mom replied and really enjoyed his experience. She said she thought it would be a great experience for me as well and if I wanted to do sports that I would have to run track.

That was it, no more questions asked. Has this ever happened to you as a kid?

In my generation kids were seen and not heard. Don't get me wrong my mom and dad were good parents. They loved me, fed me, put a roof over my head, clothed me and disciplined me when needed. In the 70's there were not many parenting classes. So they did what they thought or knew was best.

Nowadays kids are taught to make their own decisions and strive to be individuals. Supported by mom and dad, some kids run their own businesses, edit the neighborhood newspaper, put plays together, make movies and help support mission organizations. Unfortunately when kids are seen and not heard, they will be heard. What I mean is whether it is positive action or negative, kids scream to be heard. They scream to be accepted and loved by mom and dad. They scream to be respected and not talked down too. They scream to be treated as individuals and are smarter than we give them credit for. I was and negative attention was better than no attention. That was I, the troublemaker.

I was diagnosed as a hyperactive kid and I was into everything and in trouble over many things. I spent many days either being spanked or grounded. Since I was the middle child, one sister older the other younger, they loved to gang up on me and help get me into trouble which really took no help at all. But, I was going to get that attention. I remember being in so much trouble that when we moved into a new neighborhood the kids didn't even realize my sisters had a brother because I was grounded for what seemed like the entire summer. Things began to turn around a bit when I was put on Ritalin. Ritalin is a drug that helped to control my wild behavior. It did wonders. It helped calm me down and relaxed and focused me on what I was doing. My schoolwork improved and my relationships improved as well however I was a restless and anxious kid and would always be hyperactive. It takes a lot for me to stay focused even today. Over time, I have learned to strive to balance that behavior so I don't drive people crazy.

Little did I realize that rebellion had been birthed on the inside of me. Since I had spent much of my childhood in some sort of trouble this became the cycle of my life and nobody had respect for a child like me that was always in so much trouble. My individual voice was squashed and overshadowed by the constant commotion of getting into trouble. Who would actually listen to this kid? Shaped by this and getting negative attention was imprinted on me.

Rebellion was not an outward lashing out, as of yet, but it was more like a shaping of attitudes and thought processes that would be hard wired into who I was and what I thought of myself and better yet, what I would eventually become. A sarcastic mouth, off color jokes and that desire for attention was a staple with me and wired into my inner being. I wasn't important, I remember thinking, what I said didn't seem to matter. So I would retreat into myself. I was just a kid and others discarded things that were important to me as not worthy of discussion. Every-time something significant would happen in my life, coupled with a non-listening adult, rebellion would mature a bit more within me.

Rebellion is more of an attitude of defiance than anything. I spent many years wanting to be heard, hoping to be heard. Since I had no voice, rebellion within me, rose up to make that voice. The voice was a suppressed scream within, like I said, an attitude of sorts and it is the path to addiction. It is a classic behavior cycle. The addiction can be anything; in this case it became porn. Since I had trouble getting positive attention from my parents as I entered into my teens another subject began to enter the picture, girls! I thought to myself, WOW!!

I began, like most all American boys to focus my attention on the female side of life. It started out innocent enough, hormones growing and bouncing around. I remember my first real kiss. It was behind the gym one afternoon with a girl named Stacey. I really had a thing for her as she played Basketball and was a tomboy, something about that just attracted me to her. I remember her soft brown hair.

I had never really touched a girl before and remember her skin being really soft. The kiss was a simple kiss at first, however the next thing I knew she was shoving her tongue down my throat. I did not expect that at all and thought it was gross. But you have to remember I was in the seventh grade and hadn't had many girl experiences yet. She made a belt for me with my name on it in her Art class, I thought, she was the cutest girl in seventh grade and I remember asking her to "go steady" with me. Going steady was just a status at the time. We explored our crush off and on, mostly I remember just playing basketball with her. But like all first crushes, it soon ended. But we stayed friends on into high school even though we went in our own direction.

During this time in my life we were attending a little church and I became pretty good friends with the worship leader. He was a young kid of 18 or so and I was still just 12 or 13. This guy drove a sweet car and played high school football, a real mentor and friend. But he had other plans for me. Over the next 2 –3 years he repeatedly molested me. The crazy thing about this is he dated my older sister, became great friends with my parents and continued to lead worship. He was so big that I could not get away from him. He called it our game, our secret. He would tell me not to say anything about our game, others will spoil it. The de-pantsing game, I remember he called it. This was all about trying to get my pants off and trying to masturbate me. I did not get this at all and became pretty confused over the whole thing. It started by him inviting me to run an errand or go to lunch with him. We would take off and everything would be great until he would pull over and start fondling me. I would struggle against him but the more I fought the more I lost. I would try to pull my pants up but he would just pull them back down as he pinned me tighter against the seat and continued to touch me. I was scared to tell anyone about it because I thought I would get in trouble and that was the last thing I needed. Remember, I was always in trouble.

The summer of 1979 my oldest sister graduated high school and I remember this summer well. My cousin flew out from California to attend the graduation. During his visit he decided to come out of the closet and announce to the family that he was gay. Well, needless to say, I freaked out, got on my bike and took off for the afternoon. When I got back home my mom wanted to know what was up. I exploded the last 2 – 3 years of my life all over. She freaked, called dad and it all hit the fan. I do not know why I did it this way but something hit me about my cousin and what was happening to me. Something just clicked, like I snapped. I never knew what happened to the kid who molested me. However I had changed. I will always ask, why? Why me, why him, why like this?

I had mixed feelings about all this. My parents never really had much to say about what happened to me. They needed to know I was alright, but during the 70's parents didn't have ways of dealing with these types of family issues like they do today. So, it became the elephant in the living room and nobody talked about it. I always thought that it was my fault; maybe it was something I did or said. I also thought it was disgusting and still do. I remember not thinking about what happened, not mulling it over or dwelling on it, over and over. I never had the chance to process through it and didn't know I needed too, I never realized that processing through it led to healing. I actually pushed those emotions to the side and surpressed them. I did what therapists call compartmentalize my emotions and for many years I never thought about it let alone talk about it. Have you ever had something in your life you just don't know what to do with? That's how I feel about the molestation. It's something I literally don't know what to do with. It just hangs out there. I don't know if I'm healed or not because I don't know what that should feel like. It's kind of like being lost. Have you ever been lost? You get panicked, you calm down, try to get your head on straight but are at a loss of what to do. It's like being in a completely dark room with no light switch and no door. There you are in total blackness with no way out, nowhere to turn and no one to help you. I don't know what to do with the molestation issue. So, for now it just hangs out there. I hope in the future I am able to come to terms with it but for some reason I can't right now and like I said, I am not sure why.

From about 14 on, like most young boys, girls were a main focus of my attention. I attended a middle school a few miles from our house. All the kids would meet at a park in our neighborhood to catch the bus. There were so many kids that rode the bus to school that we were split up. We had one girl's bus and one boy's bus. One day a friend brought his brothers Penthouse to the bus stop. I remember being fascinated with the pictures as most of us were. This has been so burned into my mind that I still remember what color the letters across the front page were, yellow! Most of us had never seen images of naked women and my obsession with this was only beginning. Many of my friends felt like I did. They just had their first impression of a naked girl. Like most boys our age I was scared to death to actually talk to a girl but now I had seen one naked. I will never forget what happened that day. I remember that none of us really said anything, almost like a hush fell over our little group. Remembering back it seemed like it wasn't a big deal but one day it would be. We all probably found that out.

Questions to Think on-

　　1. What makes an addict?

　　2. How do we begin the change?

　　3. What role does personality play in the developing addict?

Chapter 2

Full Blown – True Addict

Addiction is a sneaky thing. I didn't know I was an addict but I knew something was not right. I couldn't put my finger on it but something just seemed out of sorts. I wasn't a very social person, I didn't have many friends and I constantly looked at women. I know that guys are visual but I looked at almost every woman that would come into my view. It seemed at times I could not get enough. What was wrong with me I thought, I've got to get this under control. Are all guys like this, I wondered?

I was about 19 when I had my first serious relationship. Lucy was her name. She had long sandy brown hair, a skinny little waist, looked great in a pair of jeans and loved rock and roll music. AC DC was her favorite band and she loved the all girl hard rock bands like Heart, as well. She was cute, small framed and soft skinned. She always wore the perfume "Poison" and I loved the way she smelled. I hadn't had hardly any experience with girls as of yet. We were both virgins when we met and about 4 months into our relationship we slept together. That in itself became imprinted in me because it was my first sexual relationship. I remember it pretty vividly as we were at her best friends parents house one night. Lucy was supposed to be house sitting while her best friend and family were on vacation. We were making out pretty heavily in her best friends bedroom and BAM, it just happened. You know when you get into the thick of it, clothes coming off and petting pretty heavily. I was a bit freaked out afterward and I think she was too. We didn't think it would actually happen as we had talked about it off and on and thought about it. She didn't think she was quite ready and I didn't want to push it. We never really set a date for it to happen, it just did. After the sex our relationship became solid as a rock, I remember, and I always wanted to have sex. I heard what it was like but never experienced it and now that I had, I just had to have more. During this time I became roommates with a friend from work, his name was Alan and we moved into an apartment. It was the first time I had been away from home and the relationship with my girlfriend seemed to grow deeper.

We hung out with friends who loved to watch porn movies. So it became a Friday night thing with us and we watched all the time. Everyone would meet at my place. They usually brought the movie. Sometimes it was girl on girl, sometimes just guy on girl. Nothing too freaky and weird just good old-fashioned hard-core sex. Some movies were in black and white which brought a different dimension to the mood in the room. I remember the sexual tension rising when we watched the movies and Lucy and I disappearing into another room for some alone time, if you know what I mean. We didn't think it was that big a deal which I found a little strange as I never had engaged in this type of activity before and I now realized how detrimental that was and that the porn addiction was maturing and solidifying within me every-time I watched; it would be like concrete, hardening in me. I believe it was now that I started to become a true porn addict.

Lucy and I broke up when she decided she wanted to date other people. This devastated me. What made matters worse was, we had the same friends and whenever we all hung out, she was there. She started dating a few of them and that was hard to take. After the break up I had moved back in with mom and dad for while and I wanted to talk to my dad about her and our break up but he just seemed to blow it off like it wasn't important. Over the next 6 months the memories of the breakup were overwhelming. We did a lot of mud slinging. She would tell her friends she wanted me back, I got hopeful and things wouldn't last. But with the support of my closer friends, I got through it but not without a price.

That price, I felt, was a hardened heart towards women. I thought to myself, never again will I be hurt that bad. From then on, I dated women for one thing, sex! Once I got it, they were gone. I didn't want anything to do with relationships after that. I did not want to become emotionally involved, put my heart on the line and get it stomped again. No way! That just hurt too much. I think this drove me into myself even more.

For the next eight years I dated on and off but was never real close to anyone. Like I said, I wasn't going to be hurt, so I put a wall up when I would start to get close to someone. They would be gone soon after and I would be single or back to finding someone to date.

Through a mutual friend I met John. Over the next several years we became good friends. He grew up a lot like I did in a somewhat normal family, had two sisters and loved the outdoors. We had a lot in common and we could talk about almost anything. One day we decided to get our own place. I didn't have a brother so he became that for me. He had always worked construction and it was a pretty solid and good paying job, so I trusted him to be a good roommate. When he moved in, his entire collection of porn magazines came with him. WOW!! You can just imagine! There wasn't a day that went by that I wasn't looking at them. Naked girls all over, guy on girl, hard core sex, vibrators and sex toys, soft porn and hard-core stuff even 3 on 3 type stuff. He had over 70 magazines and this just fed the monster inside and the addiction got worse. I swore to myself, this is it, the last day I would look at this stuff. A few days would go by and I'd be back looking at them again. For almost 2 years this went on. It was a battle over porn that raged off and on in me. I felt like I was losing my mind. I truly wanted to stop but just couldn't!

A few months after John moved in we hit the bar scene. For over a year and a half we spent at least 4 nights a week at the bar and had many friends that we hung out with. Dancing, drinking, partying and late nights became the norm. I dated a lot of people but wasn't stupid either. I was pretty selective with who I got serious with. Getting serious to me meant sleeping together. Again, I never got attached emotionally but just wanted the sex. I remember it got so bad, that at one time I dated a girl who got very serious about wanting to make our dating into a long term relationship. She would follow me everywhere. She would show up at our place at 3 in the morning pounding on our door wanting to talk to me.

But this is what my life had become. People were coming and going all the time and our place became more of a crash pad than a normal home to live in. If we weren't partying at the bar we were throwing parties down at the river. The people John and I hung out with enjoyed dirt biking and four wheeling, so every weekend was filled with some sort of four wheeling adventure and party. We would hang out on a sand bar, kegs in the backs of our trucks, rock and roll blaring out of the speakers. This is how our Sundays were spent, racing our trucks through the river and dirt biking all day. I loved dirt biking! I pretty much grew up in the outdoors and it was one of the best hobby's I had ever been into and had many friends that were into it as well. We would take off for half a day just exploring! However, this kind of life was getting old. It was getting way too crazy for me and I had enough. I told John I needed out, 2 weeks later I was gone, living in Texas with my sister, just to get some sanity back in my life. It wasn't a difficult decision. I needed space, I think I was starting to grow up and become an adult. Putting my life together was becoming more important. I knew I couldn't spend the rest of my life in the party zone. John didn't understand and was pissed off at the thought of me moving out. He handled it well however and was a real trooper helping me to get moved. He stayed a few more weeks at the apartment after I had left but eventually would move in with his Grandmother.

I didn't date much in Texas. I lived there about a year. Mostly just wanting to get my life back together, get some bills paid off and take a break from everything that had happened back home. Texas was great. I made some good friends and lived a much healthier life. I found a job with an electronic company making good money and worked with them for about a year. The company began to experience some financial issues and soon rumors were swirling about layoffs. Since I was a single guy I decided to take a voluntary layoff from the company and move back home. It was good to be home, I thought, so I found a new job, began working and met a great girl, her name was Katie.

We were a blind date, set up by a mutual friend and Katie wasn't like anyone I had ever dated in my life. I dated girls who had no goals and not much of a future. This was not who Katie was. She was serious about life, loved to travel and learn new things, graduated college and was going places. I could see that this was the girl for me. She was pretty and sweet. She looked great, had long hair and smelled good. She was soft skinned and had beautiful deep eyes and she was so easy to talk to. She was a lot of fun to hang out with and we would talk about life for hours. She was the whole package. Something I'd been looking for. We dated for about 6 months and moved in together and 8 months later we were married.

As newlyweds we decided to subscribe to Penthouse to spice up the sex life, thinking it would be great. Thinking back it was probably a mistake. Each time I read or looked at Penthouse the addiction seemed to solidify deeper within me locking me more inside myself. I really couldn't talk to anyone about the way I felt because I thought they would think of me as a freak. The more I kept it inside the worse it seemed to get. Ever felt like that before? Then a cycle of shame and guilt would wash over me. What was funny was before I was married I didn't feel guilty or shameful. But now I felt like I was cheating on Katie and in my mind I was. The shame and guilt would eventually ease up but the next time I spent time with that magazine, there was the shame and guilt all resurfacing again. I hated that and could not seem to get away from that feeling. I mean Katie was my love and what I truly wanted in a women and I felt like what I was doing with the magazine took away from what we were suppose to have. Getting married means that you have decided to have that exclusive special relationship with someone you want to spend the rest of your life with, right? At times, I truly felt like I was cheating on Katie and I think this is where the guilt and shame came from. Something inside me knew it wasn't right but I needed a fix, I couldn't get away from it and the harder I tried, the worse the addiction seemed to get.

We fought for the first year or two of our marriage. Looking back I think it had a lot to do with the roles we were trying to fit in as husband and wife. I mean nobody sits you down and discusses the roles you need to play; you just figure it out as you go. It was like vying for power. How would we pay bills, who would fix dinner, clean the house and yard, wash the car, simple things that make a household work. What exactly did the husband do, and what exactly did the wife do? We both had great jobs, no kids, 2 dogs and a cat. It seemed to be all about running the house. We were pretty selfish as well. Money did not seem to stretch as far as we wanted it to. I placed some hard-core demands on Katie and remember when she came home with what she thought was a great raise. Instead of praising her for doing such a great job and recognizing the reward for it, I wanted to know why the raise wasn't for more money. How sad, looking back on that. I treated her as a commodity and not a human being.

However, this was how we treated each other. Inside I knew I needed help and our marriage needed help but where could we turn? I had no idea.

Questions to Think on-

1. How should we treat our wives or husbands?

2. What do you think the change process will look like?

Chapter 3

Porn Dude vs Jesus Christ

I worked for Intel Corporation for 8 years. It is a great company and for most of the time I enjoyed my job. I was frustrated however with my marriage, Katie and I seemed to be butting heads more and more. I started hanging out with a girl at work a little too much. A co-worker named Brian called me out one day and wanted to talk to me. Brian was a great guy, hard worker and later would become a good friend. He told me he had been praying for my marriage because he noticed that I was hanging around Tina. I said that's really great but in my mind thought it was a bit weird. I mean I never really thought about God or church except for once in a while. In my mind I knew I was a good guy and with that thought I knew I had to be one of God's favorite people. I didn't have any hard evidence to go on here but I knew I was right so, what could happen? I never really had anyone approach me to tell me they were praying for me and I didn't know too much about heaven or hell. I mean, I was young, just married, life was pretty good. I was making good money, had a nice car and house, why did I need God?

Brian invited Katie and I to the church he and his family attended. I said we would talk about it but could make no promises. Then one Sunday we decided to go on a whim. I distinctly remember when we got home there seemed to be this peace that was raining down on us. I can't explain it but this Sunday Katie and I were at peace with each other. I mean you have to think about this, peace wasn't a word in our household. The buzzword was pins and needles, if you know what I mean. Once or twice a month for the next 6 months we attended this church. I am not sure how this came about but one day we decided to do this church thing full time. I think we decided that if it was going to help ease the fighting between us then we were all over it. So we met with the pastor and told him about our plans. A few Sunday mornings later we were baptized together and made Christ the king of our marriage and our lives. We made many friends and really enjoyed our decision and the church. However the porn thing didn't go away. I had hoped it would, but no. I still battled the demon within. I thought many times how can Jesus love me when a battle like this brews inside of me and I feel like this. Have you ever felt like this?

Through Brian I met Thomas. Thomas, Brian and a few other guys met after work every week or so and studied God's word. I was invited to join them and eventually Thomas and I began to meet one on one to study how to live a Christian life. I mean, I had lived all my life in the world, I knew how to take care of myself, but learned God wanted to take care of me and created me for fellowship with Him. So I spent time studying God's amazing word and learned much about how He sanctifies us through His spirit and His word. Paul discusses this in depth in Romans. Even though I read this I just couldn't get my head wrapped around it. I couldn't quite understand but knew that through His son and His spirit He slowly cleans us up. That's all I knew at this point, I don't really know how He does it, as that part seemed to get lost between my head and my heart. I mean I know what His word says but I wasn't living it and this made me crazy.

When I first met Jesus the porn issue seemed to dissolve to a small spark. Don't get me wrong here, I still struggled but the fight didn't seem so intense. So, I really didn't think the porn thing was a big issue with God. Maybe He doesn't know about it, I thought and maybe He wouldn't bring it up. Whoa, did He have other plans! Funny how that happens.

Katie and I started doing some volunteering with the youth group and became good friends with the youth pastors. The youth pastor and I would become like brothers. Like me, he loved the outdoors, hiking and mountain biking. It was March of 2000 when he and his wife announced that they were moving to Denver to start a church. This had been welling up inside them for quite sometime and they had finally made a decision that this is what they sensed God was doing in their life. Over the next 8 months or so Katie and I would begin to pray in this area of our life. We sensed a deep connection to these two people and sensed that the vision God had imparted into them we could possibly support.

In September of 2000 he and his wife moved to Denver and March of 2001 Katie and I followed. We loved the Denver area. It was the big city and much different than Albuquerque, where we were from. The Rocky Mountains were amazing and we had never seen mountains quite like these. If you haven't seen the Rocky Mountains you are in for a treat.

They are amazing to look at and even more amazing to camp in. Denver has Coors field, the Bronco's and the Denver Nuggets basketball. Man, what more could you ask for!!

It was great being friends with Tim as he was the first person in my life I could really talk to about the porn issue. I mean really get down to the issues! He seemed to understand and not judge me. In fact he struggled with the same issue. I thought WOW someone I can identify with. Someone who knew what I was going through and actually understood it, like a brother. We seemed to feed off each other in this area and help each other through the difficult times. However, after about 2 years the new church plant closed its doors and he and his wife moved out of the area to live with family. It seemed after the church closed the addiction became worse than ever. Over the next year or so I battled depression as well as the addiction itself. I do not know why this became fiercer and fiercer but I began to see it was a spiritual battle. Looking back I truly believe that God was in a battle with satan over control of my heart. It got so bad that I remember being on my knees crying out for Him to take this away. I felt lost, and filled with more shame and guilt. I was truly disgusted with myself and the way I had been acting. This is when I decided that I really needed to put the porn thing behind me and try to get myself back on track but really didn't know how. I learned that every bible verse you quote during this battle will not help if you don't understand that you need wisdom to see where the battle started. I was truly in the dark for any understanding of the addiction. So, I began to ask that God would give me wisdom and insight as to why this continued to happen, where this came from and why it was such a battle. I knew that a Godly man that loved Christ as much as I did could not continue down this road.

I went through periods where I felt like I was the biggest hypocrite out there because I was striving to live my life for God, but knew that my heart was filled with this death. I hated feeling like this. The battle was very intense and the guilt and shame were overwhelming. Finally, we cancelled our Internet at home. That seemed to help but the issue didn't go away. I began finding opportunity to surf at work when no one was watching. I couldn't help it because I needed a fix! It didn't matter where I turned it seemed to be there taunting me, calling out to come and play. I felt like someone or something was pulling me apart at the seams. Again, how could Christ love someone as filthy and filled with hypocrisy as me? Through all this I think Christ's word began to come alive in me and I began to see that Christ loves these types of people just as much as others without these issues. I mean, He hung with prostitutes, drunkards, tax collectors and more. This was His ministry; this was His mission, the mission that God gave Him. He came to help people just like me. That began to seriously resonate within me. I began to think okay, if Jesus could hang out with people as messed up as this, he could help me and by His grace, He did.

His grace works like a father who yet again catches his son or daughter doing something wrong. It could be a lie, or bullying a sibling, maybe fighting, whatever. A father might punish his child somehow, but mostly a loving father wants his child to learn why this behavior is wrong. A father doesn't just condemn his kid or turn his back on them; he works with him to help him understand why the behavior is not right. God doesn't just want you to quit the destructive behavior; He wants you to know why and will help you figure it out in order for you to get there. God loves and cares for those He created. Now, its up to us to change that behavior.

One morning I was dreading going to work yet again because I knew I would be surfing porn. I was talking with Katie about the issue and she told me "why don't you look for a counselor that specializes in this area"? So, when I got to work I looked for just that and a week later made an appointment to talk to someone because at this point I was putting my family and job in jeopardy by spending way to much time surfing the web on porn sites. It was literally killing me inside but I couldn't stop. I needed that fix and the addiction needed to be fed. The more I fed it the worse it got and I was at a breaking point. I guess this is what scared me. I had heard about pedophiles and sexual predators and I did not want to become one, but left on my own I could have easily gone there.

Questions to Think About-

1. Does an addiction get more intense as we get older?

2. Are there people in your life with this addiction?

Chapter 4

A Counselor?? Are you Kidding?!

You have to understand that I wasn't thrilled to be going to a counselor. I mean, who would be? Most people want to try to solve the issue on their own. But that just hasn't worked for me over the years. I also think one reason I didn't want to go was I really didn't want to change or maybe I was scared. I had all these questions like "do I really want to put all my dirty laundry out there for someone else to listen to"? What would my life look like on the other side, without porn"? "What if people found out, people I didn't want knowing"? "Can I trust a counselor to keep things confidential"? "How am I going to pay for this"? "Is it really worth it"? Probably the same questions you have asked. I went through them all. But, as I looked at my past, I had to ask myself this question as well. "How is my life working for me"? To tell the truth, it wasn't. The hidden side of porn was tearing me up and the more I tried to control it the worse it got.

So, I really had to think about what was more important to me- my wife, my family, my job or porn? Think about it, I have had this issue since my teens. That is close to 30 years! Part of me had learned to love porn; our relationship can be really sweet. Drinking in the images, the pictures can be exciting, thrilling and naughty. There was a part of me that liked the thrill of forbidden fruit or the tease. Watching the porn download, looking at the naked women. One image would show them completely clothed, the next image would be with a shirt off, the next with pants off and they would be standing there in bra and panties. Then, in the last images, they would be naked or with their bra off maybe even with their panties off. Some images were girl on girl kissing each other or parts of their bodies; other images would be two guys on a girl, all completely naked, kissing each other or having sex. Some images were girls using vibrators on different parts of their bodies. Some images showed girls holding their breasts showing off for the camera. Part of me liked the challenge of trying to get away with something that I knew was wrong and I thought I don't really need to change, do I? Maybe I can handle it on my own, has it really gotten this bad, I asked myself? Reality kept trying to hit, so I was in this tug of war. Should I, shouldn't I? Been there? It really sucks! Since I had made the appointment for a week out or so, it gave me a chance to think about it over the weekend and to tell you the truth, I almost didn't go. Eventually I thought, "I guess it won't hurt".

After my first meeting, I realized that what I was going through was a classic case of denial. Man, I hate that word! Denial keeps many people right where they are. Spinning their wheels and caught up in the stronghold of the addiction that holds them for years. I knew something was amiss and I knew what I struggled with through my life, but denial kept me from truly understanding that there was a possibility that I could be a porn addict. Denial can be very destructive. It is the cause of many people thinking they have no problem at all. Denial keeps people in that should I, shouldn't I tug of war and I would struggle with denial through the first month of counseling.

My first meeting was with a counselor named Steve. He gave me a set of questions to answer. Questions like "Were you sexually abused as a child"? or "Are you worried that someone might find out about your sexual activities"? There were actually 25 questions that helped Steve understand if I was a sex addict or not. Even though practically every single question pointed to a resounding yes, I still didn't quite believe that I could be addicted to sex or porn. I felt humiliated and ashamed to be at the first meeting. It was somewhat overwhelming and I thought to myself, "no way, will I ever come back". Then Steve wanted me to take a workbook and start working through the pages. I thought, "homework, are you kidding me"? It's enough that I have to air my dirty laundry out there but homework as well? This was pushing the limit! However, the next conversation helped ease the anxiety a bit. Steve and I had discussed what denial was and suggested I needed to look at the situation from the perspective of others such as a boss or family members. Try to see what they would think if they knew the severity of the problem. I thought every male looks at porn but that doesn't mean they are addicted to it or does it? I felt more relaxed as Steve continued to probe for information and discussed the possibility of group therapy. I thought, if other guys can do this, I guess I can try to give it a more positive shot.

Steve then set me up with group therapy. This is where guys with the same issues come together and discuss the problem.

The first group meeting I went to there were 4 of us guys as this was a new group just starting out. The group helped me see that there were others like me that had some pretty major porn issues. Some of the guys were separated from their wives and on the verge of divorce. Some were leaders in their church and they couldn't tell anyone and were dealing with heavy guilt and shame. These guys helped me see that not only are there sex addicts in the world, but that yes, I really was one and after a few more sessions with Steve, more questions about my past, understanding the sexual abuse, I began to see how big the problem was and couldn't quite believe they actually had a name for it. They have much more, I found out. There are sexaholics anonymous groups. This is a recovery program for those wanting to stop their sexually self-destructive thinking and behavior and these groups are filled with guys striving to make a difference in their own lives, relationships and marriages by getting the help that is out there. These groups offer a safe place for men to share what they are doing about their addiction, how they handle it and how they're moving through to freedom. A few of the guys in my group were actually in what they call an SA group which is the same as a sexaholics anonymous group. One guy who had been in counseling for a few years was the veteran of our small guys group and attended a pretty hard core SA group at a church. I found out that many churches in cities across the US offer and support SA groups. Some groups are huge, ranging from 50 to 90 guys. Some meet once a week and some meet everyday of the week. If you have ever been to an Alcoholics Anonymous group, SA is structured much like that. SA operates on a very confidential basis and anyone who attends can be assured that his or her anonymity will be protected. I didn't participate right away in our small guys group because I was new and wanted to feel I could trust the other guys however I was asked to make a commitment to the group and needed to be there every week. I began to really identify with these guys, their needs, their emotions and where they were at in their life with the addiction and after about 3 weeks I began to open up more about my own issues.

It was encouraging to see that some of them have been in this battle as long as I have and seeing that gave me hope. What was even more astounding is when I began to share my story with them, they were all there, supporting and understanding what my struggles have been. All in all counseling hadn't been too bad. It was opening my eyes to the reality of what I was and the stuff I have struggled with the past 30 years. One day I began to talk to Steve about the sexual abuse. This was really tough because I hadn't ever talked about it. I remember driving home with tears coming down my face because it hurt so much to drag that issue up. I had always asked why? Why me! Have you ever asked that question? It is a question that seems to constantly haunt me. But now, I was beginning to look at the abuse face to face and I didn't want to. It just hurt too much and still does! It was so much easier to leave it lie dormant. I had so many feelings bouncing around on the inside of me I really didn't know how to deal with it all. I still don't at times. Steve wanted me to share this in our group. It took a while for me to get there but eventually I opened up and let it all out. I told them how it all started, what happened, the acts of masturbation and the secrecy. I told them how I got pinned down and couldn't get up! How mad and upset it made me. Looking back on that day I remember how freeing it was and I learned that some of the guys had gone through the same types of sexual abuse. We all wanted to band together and kick our perpetrators asses. It was pretty awesome actually and helped me come away a bit more healed over the issue, I think. But I really don't know if I will ever be completely over it. I mean it truly is innocence lost. Part of my life will be gone forever! I think this is why I have a hard time trusting people. Why should I when I know what they are capable of? What happened to me took that part of me and I never knew how to develop trust with people. I look back at it and it really sucks. I still have all these emotions about it and don't really know what to do at times. However, my counselor suggested I write a letter to the guy who did this to me. It is part of the healing process. I really didn't want to at first. The letter is more about how I feel than anything, so I tried and this is what I had to say:

Hello Sam,

I haven't talked to you in so long, where to start? I thought we were friends. I thought you liked me and wanted to be my friend! What happened? Why did you do this to me? Why did you pin me down and over power me and molest me time and time and time again! Do you know how that makes me feel? Do you care? I can't trust people because of you. You never explained or apologized, just disappeared. I hate you! I hate you! I hate you! I hate you! You suck for what you did! I cry and don't even know why? I get depressed and don't know why. I feel like I am locked in a room with no way out. The light is off and its dark, completely black, no one is there to help me, to save me from your hand! There is no light switch. I scream but no one can hear me. Just your face I see. I think about what you did, how you took my pants off and touched me. You said it was a game and I should tell no one. You paralyzed me with fear. I became anti-social because of what happened. Sometimes I feel you touching me, get off me I scream, get off me, get off me, get off me, get off me, get away from me, get away from me!! I hate you! I feel lost! No one is there to find me, to help me, to bring me back. What do I do, where do I go, who will listen? I am lost. You suck! Sometimes in my mind I see you trying to molest me, trying to use me, trying to take from me again! Haven't you taken enough? What more do you want? I am haunted by what you did! Why? Why? I always ask, why? What were you wanting? Did you like little boys? Girls didn't do it for you! I'm lost with no way back. Out there standing in the rain. Who will say they love me, when will it all end? When will it all end? When will it all be over? Never, I get to live with this until I die! Lucky me, a ball and chain to drag around. Another set of baggage to add to what I already have! My face staring at the sky. Rain falling on me, black clouds hover over me, lightning strikes and I have no where to run, no where to go, I am lost. I don't know if I have forgiven you. Should I? I think I should. I don't know if or when that will happen. What do you think? What do you have to say? How many more have you taken from? User of people. I hate you! Every healed memory leads to another opened door. What else did you do to me? I will find out, as time reveals the memories and pain.

Writing this letter brought up a lot of pain again. Tears rolled down my face again. At times I feel bad for him, at times I hate him, I am irrational, restless and filled with anxiety now. This is what happens when I try to address the issue. I quit thinking about it and life slowly returns to normal even though I still feel anxious.

I can't explain however, how good it felt to have the support of other guys going through the same thing I was. We were becoming good friends, accountable to one another and had each others phone numbers so when we got into a bind we could call and discuss what was going on. Some would call just to discuss the fight they had with their wife, or the fact that someone had just been let go of their job, everyday stuff that makes life go around. But in our case the stress of life and family can drive us back to our escape, which is the addiction. We all tried to be there for each other. I remember, I was still porn bingeing on the computer at work and my goal, like everyone, was to try to become sexually sober. We all had certain days where we had tried to stop our sexual activities and strive to become normal again. That was real tough. But slowly through counseling and attending the group this would begin to change.

Questions To Think About -

1. What fears keep us from seeing a counselor?

2. Would our lives change if we decided to see a counselor?

3. What did they do to you?

Chapter 5

Lust Train

Lust is a human emotion that relates to sexual desire. Like all emotions our lives seem easier when they are not running out of control. Lust can run out of control like a train. Think about this. Lust, like a train, starts out slow. As we read sexually charged magazines, surf porn sites, watch porn DVDs or anything related to unhealthy sex, it will slowly build momentum on the inside of us. Like feeding coal to a train's engine, or upping the power. It takes time to build momentum but if lust is left unchecked and able to run out of control like a train it will soon crash. The crash in a sense is the addiction to sex or porn.

For me, a typical addict, my whole system screamed out that I was going to die if I didn't take a "drink". Drink in this context means a look and it's too fearful not to drink because lust became my spiritual life support system. I got hooked on it and remained a slave to it. It's this kind of fear that kept me in bondage and forced me to keep slipping with lust. I stayed in this bondage to lust because I thought I would die. I was unable or unwilling to connect with the life giver instead.

This was where I was at as I had always lusted and never really knew I needed to love nor really knew how to love. Especially when my first girlfriend and I broke up, I didn't want to get hurt again so I reverted to the fact that I could control the relationship even though

I didn't quite get this at the time. Remember how devastated I was when we broke up? What I developed, was to have a relationship I could control, that was the one I had with porn. This is why lust was out of control in my life. When we get hurt we tend to move in a direction that will not hurt us again. Some people resort to drugs or alcohol, me, I resorted to porn. It had everything I was looking for but without feeling. I didn't want the emotional impact, just the sex, because I was not going to be hurt again! Who would? Getting hurt sucks and if we are hurt by a break up we will usually not be hurt again. Our attitudes change towards the next lover and we will always have our guard up. I did. That's why I resorted to porn, porn never hurt me, or so I thought!

So, my drug became the compulsion of the look, the fantasy, image or misconnection which when denied is the very threat of death. So, instead of learning to act against the fear, to lean into the fear, I would look.

Have you ever heard of the three second rule if you've looked over 3 seconds you are lusting. Most of us think that lust has to do with timing but it doesn't at all. Lust has to do with our hearts intent. If the intention is to take a quick look, does it really matter how long we look? The intent becomes what we are and we need saving from that or the disposition of our heart.

I thought "I shouldn't be doing this" as I went ahead and took the drink. This began to show me I didn't fully understand the nature of what I was dealing with and under-estimated the strategies of spiritual blindness and denial. I did not realize that lust is a disposition of the heart or an attitude. If our attitude is to look at women as our sisters would we look lustfully? If our attitude is to look at them lustfully and we have learned that through society, how do we change or better yet, do we really want to change? Have we become so bad, so corrupted that we attach our manhood to how many women we look at this way or sleep with? What are we teaching our sons? How do they view women, like our wives or daughters?

What are we letting society teach them about women? What are they believing? Are there things, we as parents can do to ensure our sons will live a healthy life and more importantly have a healthy sex life?

Experts say that children are the most impressionable from the ages of 8 to 14. What will we impress on our sons during these ages?

I believe, that because I never had the chance to truly understand what lust was, I never had a chance to realize how bad it could get. Since I was really hurt by my first real relationship, I put a wall up so I would not be hurt again. But sex is our life support, it is what we are created to do, it is a natural human need. Nobody really discussed sex with me and because of a misunderstanding of what it was, lust in my life became totally out of control and the more I looked at porn the more out of control lust became. This was the vicious cycle of addiction. The more you look the more you need.

Lust works like most of our emotions, if we do not keep them in check they will run amok and so will our lives. My parents did what they thought was right. Lust and porn were not as big an issue as they are now and my parents did the best they could with what they had to work with and what society gave them at the time.

In my experience, I believe there are a few things that we can do to help ensure our children can have healthier relationships.

1. **Listen.** I really wish my parents had listened to me more because I believe if they had it would have validated me and helped my self-worth become much more positive. As adults we tend to brush our children's needs aside, when we do this it devalues them as individuals. Just because things that are important to them are not as important to us, doesn't mean we tune them out. They see that and it greatly affects their self-worth. A low self-worth means a low value in ones self. A low self worth leads them to think they are not worth the time to other people and can lead to unhealthy relationships.

2. **Talk about sex.** My parents never talked to me about sex. I know, really?? You say! But they never really did. I never had a chance to understand the guy's point of view as I learned it all from my friends. Do we want our kids learning about sex from their friends? We will need to start out with age appropriate topics and as they get older discuss things more in detail. Share with them how boys and girls work, how they communicate, how they need and want to be treated.

3. **Teach your kids how to treat each other.** Love your neighbor as yourself is a great golden rule. If we lead with this behavior in our homes, you might be amazed at how kids pick up on this and begin to treat their friends.

4. **When our children get in trouble, explain to them why they are in trouble**. Kids need explanations and too many times, we as parents don't take the time to tell them. Tell them why the bad behavior is not appropriate and walk them through how they need to change it. If this includes a punishment of some sort, then punish. I got some explanations when I got into trouble but I never understood my behavior and why I was a wild kid. Explanations are powerful in helping kids grow into themselves and understanding who they are. It helps their self- worth and teaches them to do better.

5. **If we invest teaching good behavior and habits** to our children, they will use what they have learned to invest in the lives of others, treating them with respect and honor.

The example we set as parents, aunts, uncles and friends will determine how our sons will treat their future girlfriends or wives and families. I truly wish I had had a mentor in my life that knew about these things and had the heart to teach a young child about relationships and sex.

Lust starts out slowly. As a child we don't even understand what lust is and definitely what it can become. If, as a child we are not guided into learning about sex in a healthy way, we take the chance of becoming a victim to lust and sexual addiction.

Sadly sex or porn addicts are some of the loneliest people in the world. As a child, I was really like this at times. It sucked not having friends, not fitting into the so called status quo and experts say that an addict's childhood is one of desperate loneliness with feelings of being lost, unprotected and out of touch. Their lives are filled with people that cannot be counted on, times when they were left by themselves and feelings of mistrust. As children mature it is human nature to search for dependency, something or someone that can be trusted. Since sex is the core of our identity many will become sex addicts. Addicts desire to connect with others but due to childhood disconnection with caregivers (divorce, abuse, neglect, abandonment) the addict attempts to fill the connection with something controllable and safe and experts say that 83% of all addicts have multiple addictions.

Since I was sexually abused for 2-3 years, I believe I lost all understanding of how to connect with adults and how to trust people. I was scared to trust people to tell you the truth. This became very apparent as I got older. I developed attitudes with people and co-workers because of this and had a hard time getting along with others.

According to Patrick Carnes Ph.D there are 4 factors in a child's development that will become part of the sexual addiction.

1. **Self-image**- How children perceive themselves. This is an important factor in the maturing child. Supporting, inspiring and encouraging children in the right direction will help them develop a healthy self-image of themselves.

2. **Relationships** – How children see their relationships with others.

3. **Children's needs**- How they perceive their own needs. Are those needs being fulfilled?

4. **Sexuality**- How children perceive their own sexual feelings. It is important for parents to communicate sex and related topics to their children.

It's easy for us to see that these items can start out healthy but if we don't make them topics of discussion with our children as they mature, these items can easily get off track, resulting in sometimes very tragic futures. We as parents should strive to have healthy and open communication with our kids. The more open discussion the better the result. We all should help children grow into healthy self-images, relationships, needs and sexuality.

Based on Front Range Counseling Centers sexual addiction guidelines, we should understand that porn sex addiction is a shame-based illness. Meaning the person receives no or little affirmation in life and has a flawed sense of self and worth. This is an intimacy disorder and many addicts have attachment issues as they don't know how to connect with others. They go through stages of isolation and self-soothing to help cope. The addiction is a problem of no attention and it is the ultimate attention deficit disorder. Addicts need the addiction to bring order to their lives and it is a coping mechanism for stress, solution to trauma and brings protection from painful memories. This is a family disease, passed down from generations of addicts. I don't know what my family was addicted to and if they ever were but I know the skeletons are there as I am reaping some of them.

My life points to an unhealthy self-image, relationships I had didn't seem to work out, and I was clueless about sex.

Understanding and familiarizing ourselves with a few of these can also help to identify a loved one who may be an addict. The sooner you can identify with them, the sooner you can help them.

Questions to Think on –

1. What do you think an obsessive luster looks like?

2. How should we treat our children?

3. Are there things you learned, that you can impress on their lives?

Chapter 6

Letting "Change" Win!

Why do we seem to sabotage our own success? Why is it that people such as our friends and neighbors can go to counseling for years yet never seem to get anywhere. Ever notice that? The co-worker that seems to have so much personal drama or a sister or friend that always seem to live for the drama yet never change despite all the advice or counseling they have gone through. Why? I believe there are several reasons. First, people like drama because they lack attention in other areas of their lives. Second, I believe that even though people talk about changing, they, like me, have a hard time getting there because that is what it is, hard. It requires personal dedication, hard work and a true desire to change a bad behavior to a good behavior.

Ever see that girl or guy with a smoking hot body? How did they get that body? It didn't just show up one day out of the blue. It took years of going to the gym and going through a personal regimen of working different parts, to get slim and muscular arms, legs, shoulders and back. Some people go to the gym all their lives to achieve that kind of body. To get a great looking healthy body it takes years of consistent work to shape certain muscle groups.

That's what it took to change my bad behavior to good behavior. Maybe not years, but I started out by striving the first week to stay sexually sober. Then working that into 2 weeks, working that into

4 weeks and so on. My first week was pretty tough, but I hung in there, received support from my counselor and turned that into 4 weeks. I admit that I slipped; I binged at times and had to start over. I got into a pattern where I couldn't stay sexually sober for more than 60 days. This went on for 6 months. Finally, I was able to turn that corner and stay sober longer. It just took a bit of dedication but having an accountability group to relate to really helped. I almost sabotaged my own change because I was lazy and didn't really want to change. The past pain of sexual abuse was tough to deal with because I never processed through what happened in the first place. That in it self almost kept me from going back to counseling and kept me from becoming sexually sober. Since I never processed through what happened, once we began discussing it, I found myself going through a range of emotions from being sad and depressed to being overwhelmed by what actually took place. That sucked. I almost couldn't deal with it all at once. But I thought to myself, I need to keep pushing through and finally, I started seeing the other side of the coin as things slowly began to change. The really cool part was once I saw the fruit of that change, I became stronger and more confident that I could actually do this.

I learned that there are actually six stages to changing a bad behavior. I never realized this and I am in what is called the action stage. The six include, pre-contemplation, contemplation, preparation, action, maintenance and exit, according to James Prochaska Ph.D, John Norcross Ph.D and Carlo Diclemente Ph.D who wrote "Changing For Good".

This great little book explores how and why people change and the six steps to change. By understanding the change process those who implement and work it will get to the other side of bad behavior and look forward to embracing positive behavior.

The porn addiction cycle really started to break loose when I started setting and putting goals in place that helped me to become sexually sober. Sexual sobriety is when I no longer needed the fix of porn to deal with past pain, anxiety and loneliness. I never realized the six stages to change but after reading just a few chapters of the book, I began to see how I had come through the first 3 stages and into the action stage. For many years I was a pre-contemplator. I thought there might be an issue but blew it off as what guys do. I never realized it was a bigger issue. I slowly moved into the contemplation stage, as I began to hit bottom and looking at porn began to dominate my life. I started to think, this is really becoming a problem, even though I didn't know what to do about it. Mostly because I thought I could still control the addiction. I learned addiction cannot be controlled. Then as I got more and more sick of myself and as the guilt and shame became more and more overwhelming, I believe I moved into the preparation stage. I wanted to gain control of my life. I wanted to be somewhat normal. I began to desire change and in my mind began to prepare that this would actually happen.

The preparation stage was a major turning point for me in the journey to gaining control over my life again. I literally became so sick and tired of what I was doing that something clicked in me and I wanted to put the whole mess behind me. This is when I began thinking seriously about going to counseling.

Right now I am in the action stage. I finally took back my life through counseling. I understood it was an addiction and took steps to become sober. I hope soon to move into the maintanence and exit stage, but I could be a few years from these last two stages.

Here are a few things I have done to help me stay sexually sober. Since the computer is my weak spot, we have password protected all Internet access at home. I have taken steps to limit 95% of my Internet access at work and password protected all work computers. I do not get behind co-workers desks without them being there or surf any computer without people present. On top of that, I mark off each day of sobriety on my calendar and set certain days as goals to shoot for. For example, I set a 3 month, 6 month, and 1 year goal and strive for those. As of this writing, I have hit my 3 month and 6 month goals and my 1-year goal. I also set weekly goals and celebrate 2 times a month when I hit every ½ month goal. I continue to meet with my counselor and have his phone number just in case I need help. I communicate with my wife about where I am in my sobriety and we celebrate each goal that I hit with something special, like going out to dinner or something that doesn't cost a lot. I do not put myself at risk by buying sexually charged magazines. I just don't go there. It's easy to walk right past a magazine rack and not look; I just had to practice doing that. I have to admit it took time making all these changes but I can taste freedom for the first time in my life, real freedom and for me that is a huge success, because of how long I have struggled with the addiction.

Porn addiction is an addiction of hiding. It is so easy to hide this addiction from people and love ones, but like me, it will eventually catch up with you. I met guys in my group who were in there 60's that had hid this addiction all their life and it was finally catching up with them and killing their relationships. Putting boundaries in place and actively working them is the only way we can be successful in staying sober.

Boundaries place a protective barrier around you to keep you from sexually acting out. Sexual addiction involves patterns of thought, association with others, and behaviors that frequently lead to sexual acting out. Boundaries help to identify risky situations or past patterns, which have been associated with acting out. To clarify ones boundaries is actually saying " I am going to take responsibility to keep myself safe by avoiding places, people, and activity's that are triggers for me and are dangerous for my recovery". To break a boundary is to head toward relapse and eventually full relapse or broken sobriety. Just like a fence protects something from being harmed, boundaries keep us from deadly influences. Choosing to stay out of "risk" situations always involves some sort of cost.

One situation that is still risky for me is getting behind a computer that is unprotected and with nobody around. This is a pretty high risk boundary that I need not to break. I strive to manage it, but it can get tough at times, especially if I am at work by myself. So, I always try to have at least one person around if I need to do something on the Internet. The littlest things can trip me up and can create a trigger that causes me to act out.

A trigger is when we sense or feel the need to act out sexually. When we begin to look at the boundaries we want to put in place we need to decide which "risk" situations we will need to avoid completely and which ones can be managed.

Sometimes putting an escape plan in place really helps. An escape plan is our own personal plan for breaking behavior patterns, when we begin to feel sexually triggered and want to act out.

Despite our best efforts to work a recovery plan we will, at times, find ourselves in the midst of sexual fantasy, and certain obsessions and possibly already doing behaviors that lead to acting out. Many times we deceive ourselves into thinking we could control the behavior on our own but reality states we cannot. Creating an escape plan will help us to see we no longer have to play the victim role but instead can take the upper hand in getting control of the behavior. When we find ourselves on the verge of acting out, it is nice to have another option. Think about these things for a personal escape plan. These suggestions come from Front Range Counseling Center and can be pretty useful.

➢ **Acknowledgement** –I try to stop and think about what is going on in my life that is causing anxiety.

➢ **Think it through** – I often try to think about, if I do this who will it hurt or what will happen after I finish.

➢ **Look inside** – What is going on inside? Am I stressed? Am I trying to avoid something? These are great questions to ask.

- ➤ **Action steps** – This is a list of steps designed to help us break out of the pattern. These might include – thinking about the effect on a victim, calling a friend, reading self-help books etc.

- ➤ **Reward yourself** – Change a bad behavior by rewarding good behavior.

- ➤ Remember that you can tailor make an escape plan, one that will fit your life style and your addiction patterns. The desire of our heart is to break the behavior pattern.

- ➤ The following staying sober review is one my counselor and I tailored made. It is unique to my set of issues but very usable for others as some of these suggestions came from guys in our group.

- ➤ Cut off or limit all Internet access.

- ➤ If the addiction is at work, see if you can cut off all Internet access, password protect computers or use a cyber patrol software to monitor use.

- ➤ Don't use the Internet unless people are around.

- ➤ Set weekly, monthly and annual goals. Celebrate when you reach a goal.

- ➤ Buy books, like some I suggest in Chapter 8, to understand the change process.

- ➤ Work the study guides you receive.

- ➤ Strive to walk past sexual magazines .

- ➤ Counselors and SA groups are a great help.

These are just a few and can change through time. What works for me may or may not work for you, but, gives an idea of how a staying sober plan works and how to set one up. A good sexual addiction counselor can help you through the process of airing out the past and putting a new future in place.

Questions to Think on –

1. What will it take for us to change?

2. Think about a plan that would work in your life.

3. What do you want your family to say about you when you are no longer alive?

Chapter 7

For Parents, Wives and Loved Ones

At this point you might be wondering what to do if you have a loved one who might be a porn addict? There are several ways to approach the subject with them.

Earlier in the book we discovered that, porn addiction is an addiction of hiding. It is a delicate issue to bring up. I believe the reason why is because it is a shame based illness. People who are caught in the act feel ashamed of what they are doing.

When I decided to tell Katie what was truly going on, her reaction was, she really didn't understand. Of course, she was disappointed in me but mostly she didn't get why I had to look at porn. She was surprised at the depth of the addiction, how secretive I had been and she was concerned that I was not upfront about the issues at hand. We both, however, were in the same boat, trying to understand how and where and why this all happened and how we could get it behind us. The beauty behind my disclosure is she never judged me for what I was doing, as I did that to myself. I already knew what I was doing, it was bad enough without having her judgment hanging over me. I think this is the biggest issue. If you can draw the issue out of the person without judging them that would be the best way to communicate. And communication is the true key to solving and coming to grips with sex porn addiction in a loved one. When I started counseling, my communication with Katie had to increase. She wanted to help me get through it and one of things I had to do was tell her every week, where I was at in the recovery process. It really helped us both get our relationship back on track. It was tough, however, telling her everything I was doing. I was really mad at myself for not being able to control the addiction, I felt out of control, alone and humiliated. Once I told her everything, however, it felt so good! Like the damn just broke and the weight was lifted off my shoulders. It was a huge relief letting it all go and letting her know, I thought I was going to be alright and we were going to be alright. Tears rolled down our faces, we hugged and cried because we knew that hopefully the worse part was behind us.

Since the addiction is shame based, the person is probably sick and tired of doing it and wants to stop but it is an addiction and they are stuck in the cycle of addiction. Helping them understand what they are doing and making them aware of it helps them understand they need to stop and get help. The more you can offer them at this point the better off the recovery will be. Some families and loved ones will even research what porn addiction is before they confront the issue at home.

What was the definition of sexual addiction? Sexual addiction is an illness of escape. Its goal is to obliterate, medicate or ignore reality.

It is an alternative to letting oneself feel hurt, betrayed, worry and most painful of all – loneliness. It is important to realize that the addiction itself is a solution to pain, past trauma and anxiety.

Katie also understands the addiction is not about her. She is a beautiful women and I love her dearly. She doesn't need to change for me. She doesn't need to be sexier or hotter or wear different clothes or makeup as I love her the way she is. The addiction was birthed in me because of things that have happened in the past. She really gets this and supports my efforts to heal 100 percent.

The following are a few things for parents and loved ones to look for when it comes to determining if a person you know has an addictive behavior. This helpful list comes from Patrick Carnes Ph.D book "Facing the Shadow".

➤ Loss of control – I felt like I was losing control of my life and I looked like it at times. Nervous, jittery, out of character.

➤ Compulsive Behaviors –Addicts may have other addictions. One of mine is a compulsive desire to check all the doors and windows at night before bed. We discovered this was a security issue within me because I never felt secure enough in my relationships.

➤ Efforts to stop –I repeatedly tried to stop. I even took specific steps to stop, which failed miserably.

➤ Loss of time – I spent significant amounts of time obtaining sex or being sexual. Other things in my life were put on the back burner because of this.

➤ Preoccupation – I was obsessing about my behavior or preparation of acting out. Preoccupation becomes a means of escape.

➤ Not fulfilling obligations – I spent way to much time online or chasing sexual activites and the behavior interfered with my work and my family.

➤ Escalation –One thing that scared me was I began to see the addiction escalating, meaning I needed it more and more and younger and younger. I also began to look at things that were really not normal.

➤ Losses – I began sacrificing important parts of my life such as work and family for the addiction.

➤ These are a few things to look for in a loved one that may help determine if the addiction is active or not. It is important to note that not all of these have to be happening at the same time.

➤ The following comes from Patrick Carnes Ph.D book "Facing the Shadow" and is very informative in determining the different types of negative sexual behaviors.

Fantasy sex is a great way to act out dreams or stuff that's in your head and many adults do this. However in an addict's life, fantasy can get way out of control.

Voyeurism happens through visual stimulation. This is what is known to most people as "peeping toms". People have been caught with video cameras outside the victim's homes, looking through windows or doors. Addiction occurs when a person is constantly doing this and the behavior is consuming their life.

Exhibitionism is when the addict wants attention from other people and will go to extremes to get it. Usually that is when he or she exposes themselves to another.

Paying for sex is another type of behavior that can get obsessive. I never did this but knew people who did. Once we get into the cycle of paying for sex it is difficult to break. It is a type of control behavior and addicts love to be in control.

Intrusive sex is all about control and domination. Like rape, it is about dominating the person.

Anonyomous sex is a very high-risk sexual behavior with unknown persons and arousal occurs immediately because it involves no cost or seduction. I never got into this but addicts long to remain unknown and will go to many lengths to remain hidden.

Pain related behaviors again are all about control and domination. Spanking, hurting, slapping and kicking all cause arousal in the addict.

Some of these behaviors such as fantasy and seduction are normal human sexual behaviors. The others are not normal human behavior but sexual activities that are out of control. However fantasy and seduction can become out of control as well.

You may say "well this is all fine and even informational but how do I know when the behavior is an addictive behavior or out of control"? Experts tell it like this, if the behavior is a secret, creating a double life, if you don't want people to know about it, if the behavior is abusive to yourself or others, if the behavior is being used to avoid painful feelings or it is empty of any emotions when it comes to a committed relationship you are probably an addict.

If a loved one expresses interest in recovery, assist them in setting up and supporting a plan that will help them make positive changes in their life. They may not be interested in counseling but they are expressing a desire to change. Finding out that a loved one is addicted can be a very surprising insight in many families. Understanding what steps to take is important in helping the person change the behavior.

The following is an example of what I believe an individual recovery plan can look like.

First, individual counseling can help bring perspective, understanding and insight to the issue. Counseling really helped me to understand the addiction, when it was birthed and why it happened. My counselor acted like a guide in my recovery process, leading me through painful past experiences and helping me to heal from the hurt. Second, there should be involvement in group therapy. Many counseling centers offer group therapy, this, coupled with individual recovery work through a set of workbooks designed to help understand sex or porn addiction can really open us up to cleaning out the past and helps to get a handle on acting out. Third, regular attendance at a 12-step SA meeting is encouraged. There are groups in many areas of the U.S. and information on the Internet of where and when they take place. Fourth, I encourage you to begin a relationship with a sponsor through an SA group. A sponsor is a mentor to an addict, someone who has been in their shoes and continues to work through their own issues as well but can be a source for inspiration and help. Fifth, the need to complete steps 1 –9 in an SA group. This will help you to become stronger and more confident in the recovery effort, lessening the chances for relapse. If I knew about these early on in my life maybe I would not be here today. I wish someone would have sat me down and helped me to understand the amount of assistance out there. It truly is amazing!

If this seems too much or overwhelming at first, think about an SA group as a starting place. Anyone who has a desire to change the behavior can attend. Just 1 or 2 meetings can open individual's eyes enough to see there is an issue.

Questions to Think on –

1. Is the problem severe enough to see a counselor?

2. Are there fears that keep us from attending an SA group?

Chapter 8

What Now?

My hope and desire is that this book would be a place for us to start healing from the pain, hurt and sexual addictions that plague our lives. It would be a start in the process of understanding porn addiction and shattering it in our lives.

For many years, I didn't even know this was a problem or an addiction. I got so sick of doing it that something had to give. The addiction had me wrapped up tight. It was like a dam that formed a crack. The crack began to leak more and more and finally a huge wave of everything that remained inside came washing out. My eyes were really opened to what I had been through as a kid and how that had so affected my adult life and all of my relationships.

Counseling really helped me understand what I had become. I was living an unhealthy life but didn't know why and through it I found freedom, education, understanding and compassion. I also found that much of what I had done was not my fault although now it was my responsibility to get straight, clean up and fly right.

I continue to learn about porn addiction because I will always be recovering. Through time the triggers will become less but I know I need to stay vigilant in my efforts.

The following is a summary of successful recovery efforts that can be put in place by you or a counselor.

Phase 1 - Timeline – WEEK 1 year to 2 years

Begin a relationship with a counselor or attend an SA group

Confront denial

Begin to work a 12 step program

Put a recovery and escape plan in place

Start looking at boundaries that work for you

Address health and legal issues

Get educated on sex addiction through self help books or a counselor

Phase 2 - Timeline 1 year to 3 years

Complete 1st step of 12-step process

Agree on and begin to work a sobriety plan

Group therapy and weekly accountability to avoid relapse

3-6 months of sobriety

Phase 3 – Timeline 2 years to 4 years

Complete 2-12 of 12-step program

Start family counseling if there is a need

Process through past trauma and pain

Receive a multiple addiction assessment

Look at addressing spiritual issue.

May want to start looking at career issues if needed

The Solution

I saw that my problem was three fold, physical, emotional and spiritual. Healing had to come about in all three. The crucial change in attitude began when I admitted I was powerless, that my habit had me whipped. I went to meetings and withdrew from the habit. For me, this meant no sex with myself, or others, It also meant drying out and not having sex with the spouse for a time to recover from lust.

I discovered that I could stop, that not feeding the hunger didn't kill me that sex was indeed optional. There was hope for freedom and I began to feel alive. Encouraged to continue, I turned more and more away from my isolating obsession with sex and self and turned to God and others. All this was scary. I couldn't see the path ahead, except that others had gone that way before. Each new step of surrender felt it would be off the edge into oblivion, but I took it! I stepped into the light, into a whole new way of life. The fellowship gave me monitoring and support to keep me from being overwhelmed, a safe haven where I could finally face myself. Instead of covering my feelings with compulsive sex, I began exposing the roots of my spiritual emptiness and hunger. And the healing began!

Listed are some awesome resources for you to research and use.

Books

"Out of the Shadows: Understanding Sexual Addiction" Patrick Carnes Ph.D

"Changing for Good" James Prochaska Ph.D, John Norcross Ph.D, Carlo Declimente Ph.D

"Facing the Shadow" Patrick Carnes Ph.D

"Falling Forward: The pursuit of Sexual Purity" Craig R. Lockwood

"Trauma and Recovery" Judith Lewis Herman

"Staying Sober" A guide for Relapse Prevention, Terence T Gorski & Merlene Miller

Recovery Groups

SA- Sexaholics Anonymous – www.sa.org

Sex Addicts Anonymous – SAA – www.sexaa.org

Celebrate Recovery – www.celebraterecovery.com

Foundations Counseling – www.foundationscounselingllc.com

Front Range Counseling Center – www.frontrangecounseling.com

Website Resources

www.covenanteyes.com

www.pureonline.com

www.porn-free.com

www.sexhelp.com

Bibliography

Carnes, Patrick Ph.D – "Out of the Shadows" Understanding Sexual Addiction" – 3rd Edition 2001, Quotes.

Carnes, Patrick Ph.D – "Facing the Shadow" 2nd Edition 2005, Quotes, Pg 27-31

Carnes, Patrick Ph.D – "Facing the Shadow", 2nd Edition, 2005, Quote, Pg-51

Front Range Counseling Center - "Escape Plan Guidelines", 2007

Front Range Counseling Center - "Recovery Guidelines for Sexual Addiction", 2007

Fair Use Disclaimer:

Several quotes have been taken from books I have read for limited use.

Fair use is a <u>doctrine</u> in <u>United States copyright law</u> that allows limited use of copyrighted material without requiring permission from the rights holders.

THE END

www.ingramcontent.com/pod-product-compliance
Lightning Source LLC
Chambersburg PA
CBHW031326290526
45784CB00014B/2239